A BEGINNER'S GUIDE TO BITCOIN 2021
Everything You Need To Know About It And How It Works

Copyright © 2021

All rights reserved.

No part of this book may be reproduced in any form or by any electronic or mechanical means, including information storage and retrieval systems, without written permission from the author, except for the use of brief quotations in a book review.

CONTENTS

Disclaimer

1. Is Bitcoin Actually Money?
2. Price Targets For Bitcoin
3. Common Bitcoin Myths
4. How To Buy and Store Bitcoin
5. The 10 Commandments of Bitcoin
6. The Bitcoin Revolution Is Here

Disclaimer

DISCLAIMER

The author and the publisher disclaim responsibility for any adverse effects resulting directly or indirectly from information contained in this book. The full disclaimer may be found at the end of this book.

1

IS BITCOIN ACTUALLY MONEY?

Bitcoin is a new form of digital money that was invented in 2009 by Satoshi Nakamoto.

People have called Bitcoin a bubble, a Ponzi scheme, and a scam. And yet here we are in early 2021, and Bitcoin is still not dead— in spite of years of obituaries. Even more surprising, Bitcoin is once again making new all-time highs.

What kind of bubble pops, and then comes roaring back a few years later? That never happened with the Dutch Tulip Bubble or the South Sea Bubble.

It did happen with Amazon. Amazon crashed over 90% in the early 2000's, and then came roaring back to new all-time highs in the early 2010's. It turns out that Amazon is probably not a bubble. It's here to stay.

Or if it was a bubble in the late 1990's, Amazon was a special kind of bubble. It was an example of the stock market trying to price in a new reality— the reality of an online bookstore that had set its sights on taking over the entire world of commerce.

Bitcoin is a similar kind of bubble. It is the market trying to figure out the fair value of a new form of money. Thus in order to understand Bitcoin, we need to understand what exactly money is and how it functions.

Many people think that only a government can issue money. But that's not strictly true. There is a shiny yellow metal that is accepted as money anywhere in the world, from New York to Paris to New Delhi to Kinshasa to

Rio de Janeiro.

Gold is such good money, in fact, that much of it has disappeared from circulation. Most of it is sitting in central bank vaults and Scrooge McDuck's swimming pool.

One can say with Gresham that bad money drives out good money. But what really happens is that the good money ends up getting hoarded and taken out of circulation.

When the early American settlers learned that some Native Americans accepted shell beads (wampum) as money, they got their hands on boatloads of shells and traded them for land. Manhattan sold for $24 worth of wampum and trinkets in 1626.

When hard money encounters soft money, it's the soft money that loses. If you store your savings in apples, you will very quickly find yourself poor. Apples are perishable, and not at all scarce. Shells are slightly better— not as easily biodegraded, but unfortunately not especially scarce. Silver is scarcer than shells, and gold is scarcer than silver.

As all of the world's cultures met and interacted over the past few hundred years, gold turned out to be the strongest form of money. It drove out and destroyed local currencies such as wampum, aggry beads, salt, and even silver.

Gold is durable (it doesn't rot or rust), divisible, portable, and recognizable— all of which are characteristics of good money. But what makes it really good money (and hard money) is that it is scarce. It is difficult and expensive to mine. Even if the price of gold goes up a lot, it's impossible to increase the supply of new gold by very much. If we were economists, we would say that the supply of gold is "inelastic."

Higher gold prices do not lead to a huge supply of new gold hitting the market. Historically, the supply of gold has increased by only about 1.8% every year. We might think of that as the growth rate of the money supply, or gold's "monetary inflation."

Contrast that with copper. Whenever the price of copper goes up a lot, the copper mines kick into high gear and produce enough new copper to dump on the market and drive copper prices back down. Something similar happens with crude oil. That's why they say with commodities that "the best cure for high prices is high prices."

Gold is different. It's not a normal commodity. Most of gold's value comes from its being a "monetary good," rather than an industrial input. Gold trades at a premium to its industrial value, because it is considered to be money all over the world. And it has been used as money for thousands of years.

Gold is a great example of something that functions like money, but that is not controlled or issued by any government. You can buy things directly with gold in some parts of the world (gold as a "medium of exchange"), but today gold mostly functions as a "store of value."

We all know that one function of money is as a "medium of exchange." It's easier to give you $200 for a wooden chair, rather than trying to figure out how many peaches from my orchard are equivalent to a wooden chair. As a maker of wooden chairs, you might not even want my peaches. Money solves the "coincidence of wants" problem. It allows for highly complex economies to develop, which would never be possible under a system of barter.

Money also functions as a "store of value." If I work hard for 30 years and deposit my savings into a bank, I would like that money to still be there when I retire. The bank needs to be secure, both from thieves and from governments that might want to seize my savings. In most countries today, governments steal from their citizens in a much more subtle way than outright confiscation. It's called "inflation."

When I was a child in the 1970's, a Big Mac cost about 65 cents. Today a Big Mac costs about $4.00 or more. We've all noticed how the same amount of money buys less stuff over time. We can call this "inflation," or just say that the purchasing power of the US dollar falls over time. The US dollar is not a good store of value over long periods of time. The same is true for the Euro, the Yen, and pretty much all "fiat currencies."

They're called "fiat" (Latin for "let it be done") currencies because they are magically summoned into existence by central banks. Ever since the Great Financial Crisis (2008-2009), central banks around the world have been printing a lot of new money. They try to hide this debasement of the currency using respectable names like "quantitative easing" or "accommodative monetary policy," but what they are really doing is not much different than what counterfeiters do.

Like counterfeiters, those who can print new money on demand (central banks) and those close to the money printer (Wall Street) benefit from it at the expense of ordinary savers. Wall Street loves low interest rates and money printing, and works closely with the US Treasury and the Federal Reserve to make sure that their addiction continues to be fed. There's a revolving door between Wall Street, hedge funds, private equity funds, university economics departments, think tanks, the Federal Reserve system, the US Treasury, and various regulators that ensures that the money printing continues. That's why Janet Yellen gets to be both Fed Chairman and Treasury Secretary— and why Jerome Powell moves seamlessly from private equity to central banking. Centralization and regulatory capture always lead to financial tyranny.

When you can summon new US dollars into existence through a keystroke on a Federal Reserve computer, the temptation becomes too great to be avoided. In 2020, the US government has been issuing a lot of debt, and the Federal Reserve has been buying most of it with freshly printed money. This is called "debt monetization," and it means that the US dollar will continue to rapidly lose purchasing power.

When you print a lot of new money, the purchasing power of each piece of money (old and new) goes down. Hamburgers, houses, and hospitals get more expensive. Inflation is like a hidden tax on everything. It is how governments and central bankers steal from ordinary people, without having to raise taxes or fire a shot. Governments that have huge debts denominated in their own currency will often debase their currencies, so that they can pay off their debts using devalued currency units.

Contrast that with gold. The Federal Reserve cannot print any new gold with a computer keystroke. Gold is truly scarce, and it is not subject to massive spikes in new supply like fiat currencies. Gold is neutral, apolitical, and not subject to the whims of central bankers. And unlike fiat currencies, gold maintains its purchasing power. In the 1800's, an ounce of gold bought you a nice men's suit, and it still does today. Two ounces of gold bought you a nice working horse, and they still do today.

When we say that gold is a good store of value, this is what we mean. A store of value is a way of transmitting wealth across space and across time. I can pay a friend in India using gold (store of value across space). I can also pay my future self or my heirs (store of value across time).

If I work hard for 30 years, I would like my savings not to be debased by central bankers. When I retire, I want to be able to afford hamburgers and maybe even steak. Storing your wealth in a fiat currency means that you will be eating dog food in retirement.

The biggest problem with gold is that it is difficult to move around. It's going to be quite expensive to ship and insure that gold that I send to my friend in India. When Germany repatriated $31 billion worth of gold from New York and Paris, it took 4 years and cost $9 million to move the gold. If a hostile government takes over your country, you cannot just put a gold bar in your pocket and hop on a plane or walk across a border without being stopped.

Gold is also difficult to store. I can keep it in my basement, but then my house becomes a honeypot for thieves. I can keep it at a bank, but what happens if the government decides to freeze my bank account? In 1933, the US government actually confiscated its citizens' gold holdings right before (surprise, surprise) massively devaluing the US dollar.

Gold is also difficult and expensive to verify or "assay." Is this a real gold bar, or has it been adulterated with copper or tungsten? It can be quite expensive to test each gold coin or each gold bar.

Gold is also difficult to divide into smaller denominations. It is very dense and expensive, and thus not good for small transactions. How do you give a person change when he buys a cup of coffee with a gold coin? Smaller silver coins were one traditional solution. But then you're stuck with trying to figure out the conversion rate between gold and silver.

Until recently, and in spite of these drawbacks, gold was the best money technology available. It wasn't perfect, but it did have the advantage that governments could not just print up more gold bars to pay their bills, and thus devalue the currency.

Gold is very difficult and expensive to mine. It requires a lot of energy, expertise, and regulatory approval to mine. As we mentioned before, the supply of gold has gone up by just 1.80% per year on average. Contrast that with the US dollar, whose supply went up 26% in just 2020 as the Fed printed more new US dollars. It's easy for the Fed to hit the print button. Mining actual gold is hard work.

Mining Bitcoin is also hard work. It requires a lot of electricity and expensive specialized computers (ASICs) to solve a complex mathematical problem. The Bitcoin miner who solves this problem first is rewarded with 6.25 new Bitcoin. This "miner subsidy" is cut in half every 4 years (2012, 2016, and most recently May 2020), leading to a supply shortage of Bitcoin.

Unlike gold, we know the ultimate maximum supply of Bitcoin. There will only be 21 million Bitcoin. This supply cap is built into the software code. Contrast this with gold: no one knows exactly how much gold is in vaults and coins worldwide. And no one knows the future supply of gold either. If Elon Musk or Jeff Bezos ends up lassoing a gold asteroid and bringing it back to earth, the price of gold will plummet. If you think this scenario is absurd and unlikely, remember that people said the same thing about Amazon and Tesla's businesses.

While it's impossible to know how much gold is on earth or in the solar system, it's easy to verify the current supply of Bitcoin if you run a full node (more on that later). Today there are 18,586,619 Bitcoins in existence. More than 88% of all Bitcoin have already been mined. Because Bitcoin is software code, it's easy to verify the current supply of Bitcoin and the future maximum supply of Bitcoin.

Not only is Bitcoin scarcer than gold, Bitcoin is also easier to subdivide (1 Bitcoin=100 million satoshis or "sats"), easier to send anywhere in the world instantly, and easier to hide. If you can memorize 12 English words, you can use Bitcoin to walk across an international border with $1 billion stored in your "brain wallet." Gold can be (and historically has been) confiscated. It's impossible to take away someone's Bitcoin, if they refuse to give you their recovery seed or private key.

Bitcoin provides digital and cryptographic security, without having to use a trusted third party. When I deposit money into my bank account, I am trusting the bank to keep it safe. If the bank fails, I am trusting the FDIC to pay me back for my losses. If I hold my wealth in US dollars at the bank, I am also trusting the US government not to seize my assets, and I am trusting the Federal Reserve not to destroy my money's purchasing power through too much money printing.

Bitcoin solves all of these problems. I can hold my Bitcoin in self-custody, and no one can take it from me. I'm not dependent on a bank or other third party. The Federal Reserve cannot devalue my savings that are held in Bitcoin. If the Fed prints more money, the price of my Bitcoin in US dollars will go up to compensate for this new money printing.

It's also easy to send anyone some Bitcoin. No one can stop me from sending it or stop you from receiving it, even if they don't like our political views. PayPal can freeze your account. The US government can freeze your assets. But neither can touch your Bitcoin.

This will become increasingly important as the US government's hostility towards private property increases. The US is rapidly moving towards socialism and MMT (modern monetary theory). There is no end in sight for government confiscation through taxes and monetary inflation caused by excessive central bank money printing.

Many people in South America, Africa, and the Middle East are already using Bitcoin to protect their savings from hostile governments. Now the world's reserve currency (US dollar) as well as the Euro, the Yen, the Australian dollar, the Canadian dollar, the British pound, and almost all other fiat currencies are being devalued at an accelerating rate by central bank money printing.

Some people like to criticize Bitcoin for being uncensorable. They say that Bitcoin is only for money launderers, drug dealers, and other criminals. However, recent studies have shown that only 1% of Bitcoin transactions are for illegal activity. The US dollar (and suitcases full of cash) is still the preferred currency of criminals. That fact doesn't stop these same critics from transacting in US dollars.

People who still think that Bitcoin is only for criminals have had a difficult time avoiding cognitive dissonance in 2020. Wall Street has been setting up funds to buy Bitcoin. Billionaires have been buying up Bitcoin for their own accounts. US regulators have now made it easy for US banks to custody

Bitcoin. PayPal has been allowed to use Bitcoin by US regulators. If the US government were going to ban Bitcoin, or if Bitcoin was only for criminals, why are US regulators allowing blue chip companies to get in on Bitcoin?

You can say that many Wall Street firms and some blue chip companies are not much better than criminal actors, and you wouldn't be too far from the truth. But that's hardly a reason not to buy Bitcoin. Wall Street is good at spotting long-term trends and riding them for profits. What is remarkable about Bitcoin is that this is the first time that the small retail investor got to the game first. Retail investors have been buying Bitcoin for years and for low prices. Wall Street is coming late to the game, and is making these early retail investors rich, as institutional money flows drive up the price of Bitcoin.

Fortunately, Bitcoin is much more than a Wall Street fad. Bitcoin is like the internet— it's a new technology that is here to stay. As we have seen time and time again over the past twenty years, new technology displaces old technology. Amazon has gutted traditional physical retailers. Netflix destroyed Blockbuster.

Bitcoin is in the process of devouring and destroying all other stores of value. Bitcoin is a superior money technology to gold, and will continue to steal market share from it until gold has been completely demonetized. In twenty years from now, gold will only be used in electronics and jewelry. It will trade like any other industrial metal, its monetary premium having been completely destroyed by Bitcoin.

Sounds crazy? This is what has always happened with currencies. Gold destroyed wampum as a currency. The gold/seashell exchange rate has gone straight up since 1626. Gold also destroyed silver as a currency. The bimetallism wars of the late 1800's were all decided in favor of the metal that was more scarce: gold. There's a reason that the gold/silver ratio has stayed stubbornly high for so many years. People who try to short it fail to understand that gold is simply better money than silver, and that the gold/silver ratio reflects this fact.

The same thing has been happening with Bitcoin. Bitcoin has been beating all other assets since its creation. The Bitcoin/gold exchange rate has gone straight up since 2009. Bitcoin has outperformed all other asset classes, including stocks, bonds, real estate, and precious metals. In 2020, we have seen multiple institutional investors dump gold and replace it with Bitcoin. This trend will continue until it is complete.

There is also a strong demographic component to this trend. Millennials and Generation Z care nothing for gold, but are extremely comfortable with digital assets, tokens, and cryptocurrencies. Gold is going the way of the fax machine.

Meanwhile, Bitcoin is eating the world. It currently has a market cap of just $500 billion— the size of a large S&P 500 company. In a few years, Bitcoin will surpass gold's market cap of $11 trillion. At that point, one Bitcoin will be worth more than $500,000. Eventually, Bitcoin's market cap should exceed the global stock market ($100 trillion) and global bond market (also $100 trillion). At that point, it probably won't even make sense to quote Bitcoin in US dollars anymore. Investors, corporations, and even governments will have already begun to measure their wealth in Bitcoin. Bitcoin will have become the new unit of account.

Everyone underestimated how dominant and all-encompassing the internet would become (it's hard to remember now, but I witnessed it firsthand for many years). The same is true for Bitcoin. Bitcoin's future is much bigger and brighter than even most Bitcoin bulls believe.

2

PRICE TARGETS FOR BITCOIN

In the previous chapter, we examined Bitcoin as a new form of money— a new universal "store of value" that functions like "digital gold." Bitcoin is good money, because it is easily divided, sent, received, stored, and verified. Bitcoin is "hard money," because it is impossible to inflate its supply. The maximum supply of Bitcoin is and will always be just 21 million Bitcoin.

Bitcoin's digital scarcity makes it the best savings technology ever invented. You can think of Bitcoin as a giant, decentralized bank in the cloud— controlled by no one, and open to everyone. It's the people's bank. It will not discriminate against you, no matter your race, nationality, political beliefs, credit history, or social media history. It will never freeze your account, drown you in fees, or exploit you like the US banking system.

Bitcoin is a wonderful way to store wealth (store of value), but it is also a wonderful way to grow wealth. Bitcoin has gone up a tremendous amount over the past 11 years, but it still has a long way to go. If you think about it, "store of value" may be the largest use case on the planet. The category is easily valued at more than $400 trillion, once you add up traditional stores of value like gold, real estate, and stocks.

As we mentioned before, there is no reason that a superior technology like Bitcoin cannot steal huge market share from traditional stores of value like gold and real estate. Just look at what Amazon did to retailers, and what Google and Facebook did to traditional advertising. Better technologies that grow and protect themselves through network effects tend to steal market share from worse technologies. If Bitcoin steals just 10% of market share from traditional stores of value, that's a $40 trillion valuation for Bitcoin, or roughly $1.9 million per Bitcoin.

That's one way to think about future price targets for Bitcoin. Another way is to use valuation models that have been developed to estimate a fair value for Bitcoin. In March 2019, an anonymous Twitter account called PlanB published a revolutionary new paper called "Modeling Bitcoin Value with Scarcity," which later he followed up with "Bitcoin Stock-to-Flow Cross Asset Model."

Both papers were widely circulated in the Bitcoin community at the time, but went largely unnoticed in the outside world. Like most revolutionary concepts, PlanB's models have taken some time to spread, but it is finally happening.

In 2020, Wall Street woke up and took notice. PlanB's papers are one of the primary reasons that there is currently a wall of Wall Street money headed towards Bitcoin. If everything plays out according to the model's predictions, there is a high likelihood that PlanB will eventually be awarded a Nobel Prize in Economics for his work on valuing Bitcoin.

To come up with a valuation model for Bitcoin, PlanB borrowed the concept of "stock-to-flow" from precious metals analysts. "Stock-to-flow" (henceforth "S2F") is a way of measuring the relative scarcity of a commodity. To calculate S2F, you simply take the existing inventory of a given commodity (e.g., all of the above-ground gold inventories stored in vaults, coins, etc) and divide it by the annual production of that commodity (e.g. all of the new gold mined in 1 year).

S2F can be interpreted as a measurement of how many years it would take to replace the existing supply of a commodity. Gold has a S2F of approximately 55, which means that it would currently take about 55 years of gold mining at current rates to replace global gold inventories. By contrast, palladium has a S2F of approximately 1, meaning that you could replace all palladium inventories with just one year of mining.

High S2F commodities are more scarce and have higher market caps than low S2F commodities. Typical commodities like corn and crude oil have a very low S2F. Low S2F commodities have an elastic supply— it's easy to increase the supply of the commodity in response to higher prices. As a result, low S2F commodities tend to be more mean-reverting in price. When the price gets high enough, a huge new supply is created which drives prices back down (as we discussed with copper in Chapter 1).

For high S2F commodities like gold, higher prices do not lead to a commensurate increase in new supply. We mentioned earlier that gold supplies have increased just 1.80% annually on average, irrespective of whether gold prices were high or low. Take the inverse of 1.80% (1 divided by 0.018) and you get approximately 55. S2F is just the inverse of the supply growth of the commodity.

Something surprising happens when you plot the S2F of a series of scarce assets like gold, silver, diamonds (admittedly artificially scarce), real estate, and Bitcoin on a logarithmic chart, along with the market cap of each:

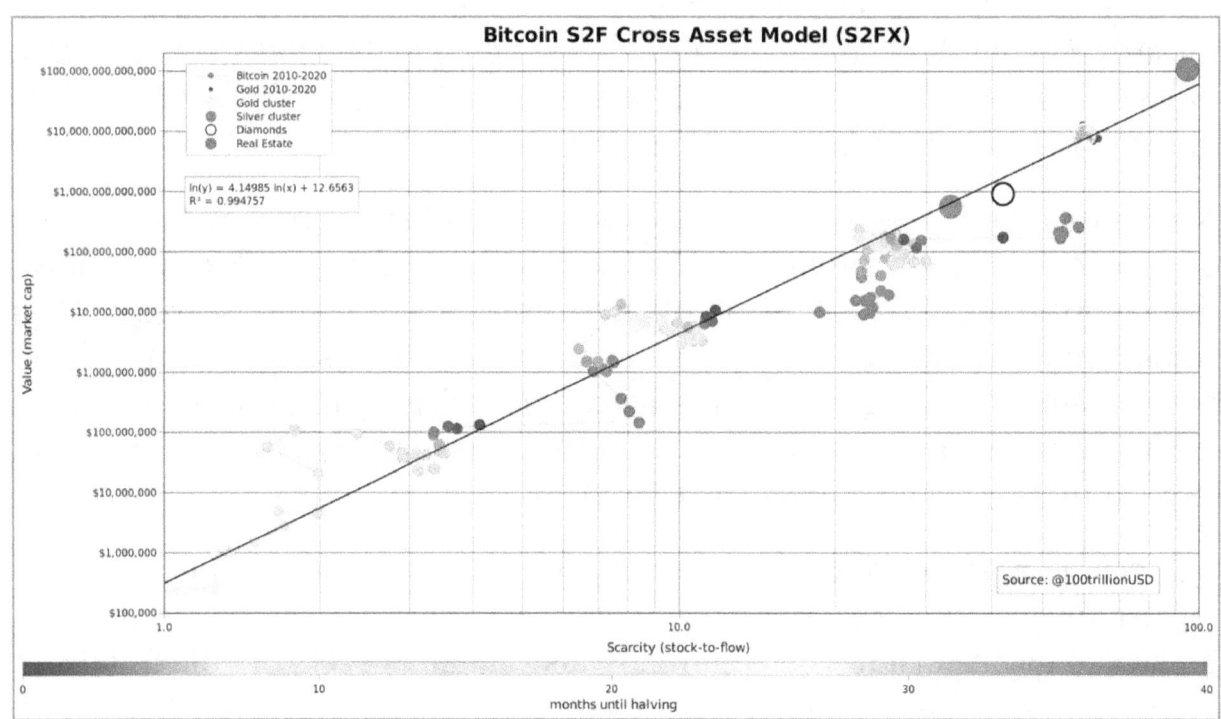

https://twitter.com/100trillionUSD/status/1338888723564474371

https://twitter.com/100trillionUSD/status/1334834429177507844/photo/1

You end up with a series of points that imply an upwardly sloping regression line. The higher the S2F, the higher the market cap of that asset. In other words, the higher the S2F, the better and more widely used an asset becomes as a store of value. This makes sense, because a high S2F implies that it is difficult to inflate the supply of that asset, and thus dilute current holders who are trying to preserve their wealth by holding that asset. As we have seen, gold has a much higher S2F than silver, just as silver has a much higher S2F than wampum. Higher S2F assets tend to beat out lower S2F assets in the "store of value" race. Hard money beats out less hard money every time.

Over time, Bitcoin itself has had different S2F values. Every 4 years (2012, 2016, 2020), the annual production of new Bitcoin gets cut in half, which causes the S2F to roughly double. In 2017, Bitcoin had a S2F of about 22, and traded at a market cap of $230 billion. After the May 2020 halving, Bitcoin's S2F has moved up to roughly 55, which puts it close to gold's S2F.

If you plot Bitcoin's S2F and realized market cap over the years on a logarithmic chart, you end up with a series of points that can be modeled using an upwardly sloping regression line. Now if you add silver, gold, diamonds, and real estate to the chart, you find that these points arrange themselves along the same line.

What PlanB seems to have discovered is a universal valuation model for stores of value. It works for precious metals, real estate, and most importantly for Bitcoin itself, in its various incarnations over the years.

It's easy to know what the S2F of Bitcoin will be in any given future year, simply because annual production of Bitcoin is predetermined by the software code itself. If we know the value of S2F for Bitcoin, we can plug it into one of PlanB's models and come up with a future market cap of Bitcoin. Divide that future market cap by 21 million coins, and you end up with the model's "fair value" for Bitcoin given a particular S2F.

Here are PlanB's model price targets for Bitcoin, as discussed in Stephan Livera's interview with him:

2021: $100,000

2024: $400,000

2028: $3,000,000

If PlanB's S2F models continue to hold up, Bitcoin still has huge price appreciation ahead of it.

There is also the possibility that institutional investors begin to "front-run" PlanB's valuation models. One of the hallmarks of the "efficient market hypothesis" (EMH) is that current information and future information that is known today will get priced into an asset. If everyone knows that Apple will beat earnings this quarter, those expected earnings will get priced into Apple's stock even before earnings are actually reported. Likewise, if everyone begins to believe that there is a 50% chance that PlanB's model will still be working well in 2028 and a 50% chance that Bitcoin will go to zero, the fair value or expected value of Bitcoin should be $1,500,000 today. PlanB's model may break to the upside, as Wall Street front-runs it and begins to price in future Bitcoin halvings today.

It's been said many times that "all models are wrong, but some are useful." In investing, it is usually very dangerous to put all of your faith in a single model or indicator. That is why I spent the first chapter of this book laying out a fundamental case for Bitcoin, drawing on first principles. Bitcoin is a better money technology than anything that has come before it, and as such it is eating the world. You can choose to believe that PlanB's models will continue to work or may fail (to the upside or to the downside). Either way, you will still have to intellectually come to terms with Bitcoin's superior technology and its rapidly growing market share. Networks grow in value exponentially as new nodes are added to the network. The Bitcoin network continues to grow and eat the world.

The strongest evidence for PlanB's models is that they have continued to work, even after publication. In finance, the publication of a trading strategy or model will often lead to a degradation of returns. Not so for the S2F models. They have continued to track Bitcoin's actual price quite well, even using the out-of-sample data that has been generated since the models were first published.

You can track the price of Bitcoin vs. the model price here:

https://digitalik.net/btc/

https://www.lookintobitcoin.com/charts/stock-to-flow-model/

3

COMMON BITCOIN MYTHS

Myth: Bitcoin uses too much energy and is bad for the environment.

Bitcoin miners do use a lot of electricity. Clickbait articles like to compare Bitcoin miners' electricity usage to that of small countries. Of course, the same critique might be made of the Internet, which uses 10% of global electricity. You'll have to decide for yourself whether cat videos and clickbait articles about Bitcoin's energy usage are a good use of global electricity. I personally think that the internet is worth it. Higher civilizations use more energy than low civilizations. If you live in a mud hut, your energy consumption will be very low. If you are part of a globally connected space-faring civilization, your energy usage will be much, much higher. Fortunately, there are nearly infinite energy sources in the solar system. Fusion and Dyson spheres will power our global civilization to the next level.

It's also unfair to criticize Bitcoin's energy usage without examining the trade-offs. Mining gold uses huge amounts of energy, and can be quite hard on the environment. The fiat financial system also uses a lot of energy. Think of all those Brinks trucks, and ATMs, and perpetually empty bank branches, with their heating and lighting costs. Printing up new paper money and coins also uses large amounts of natural resources and energy. Then there is the financial cost of human energy that is confiscated through monetary inflation.

No one criticizes a bank or brokerage (or Fort Knox) for using a lot of energy to secure wealth. You cannot just leave gold bars out in the open— they require physical security. Bank and brokerage accounts also require digital or cryptographic security, both of which use electricity.

Bitcoin is the most secure bank in the cloud. It is secured by real work carried out by Bitcoin mining computers. The high hash rate of the Bitcoin network (and associated high energy costs) ensure that it is a safe and secure place to store wealth. Bitcoin is a scarce, decentralized, seizure-resistant, and censorship-resistant way to store value. Why should something like that be free or low cost? Would you ever consider using a low-cost solution to secure a Picasso painting or the Hope Diamond?

In addition, a lot of people don't realize that a substantial amount of Bitcoin mining is powered by renewable energy (solar, wind, hydropower) or "stranded" energy sources. Stranded natural gas is often flared or vented into the atmosphere, if it is not cost-efficient to build a pipeline to move the gas. Rather than being wasted like this, there are now companies who are using this stranded natural gas to power Bitcoin mining machines.

Myth: Bitcoin is a bubble.

As we discussed in Chapter 1 with reference to the Tulip Bubble and South Sea Bubble, there has never been a bubble that popped and then came back to new highs just a few years later. People who don't have a lot of experience with markets will often call a particular market a bubble. Observers have been calling the California housing market a bubble for the past 50 years, and yet housing prices continue to march higher almost every year. Amazon was called a bubble, but turned out to be simply one of the best businesses of all time. Just because an asset like Apple or Amazon goes up a lot in price does not mean that it is a bubble.

Now that Bitcoin is once again hitting new all-time highs, the burden of proof is on the critics. What would they need to see for their hypothesis to be falsified? Peter Schiff has been declaring that Bitcoin is a bubble since 2013, when it was trading at $375. Why would anyone continue to listen to him?

Myth: Bitcoin is a Ponzi scheme or scam.

Bitcoin is completely decentralized. It is not controlled by one group, but rather control is spread across the community of miners, full nodes, developers, and Bitcoin holders. It's not like XRP, which was issued by a centralized corporation that is now being sued by the SEC. For something to be a Ponzi, you need a central ringleader like Charles Ponzi or Bernie

Madoff. Most serious Bitcoiners will tell you that they will never sell their Bitcoin. This is not how pump and dump schemes generally work.

Myth: Bitcoin is just for criminals.

Simply not true. US regulators now allow US banks to custody Bitcoin. Anyone can buy Bitcoin using PayPal. Billionaires and blue chip corporations are moving their cash into Bitcoin. Anyone who says that Bitcoin is just for criminals has not been following the news. Bitcoin is now a mainstream asset, which anyone can hold.

Now this does mean that there are no bad actors who use Bitcoin. Because there is no centralized authority who decides who can and who cannot use Bitcoin, anyone can use it— for good or evil. Just like anyone can use fire or a chemical compound for good or evil. That being said, the bulk of the world's illegal and illicit activities are still carried out using US dollars. Cryptographers, software developers, and other nerdy types who like Bitcoin usually lead fairly boring and law-abiding lives.

Myth: The government will ban Bitcoin.

The U.S. government is certainly not going to ban Bitcoin anytime soon. Bitcoin will be regulated and taxed in the U.S., but not banned. A country that bans Bitcoin is like a country that bans the internet. It will lose its best and brightest and wealthiest, who will move to a more friendly jurisdiction. As we mentioned before, you can take your Bitcoin anywhere in the world that you want, using nothing more than a "brain wallet." If the U.S. eventually bans Bitcoin, there will be a friendly country somewhere (Cayman? Singapore?) that will do everything that it can to attract those displaced Bitcoiners. What country doesn't want wealthy and educated immigrants?

The Bitcoin software is currently being run on more than 11,000 computers around the world:

https://bitnodes.io/

A government can try to shut down all of the full nodes inside of its border, but how can it shut down the full nodes that are operating in another country? If the U.S. decides to ban Bitcoin, it can try to shut down all full nodes in the

U.S. But the Bitcoin network will keep running in other countries. China and Russia might just decide that they don't want to go along with the U.S. and ban Bitcoin. A lot of other countries resent the "exorbitant privilege" conveyed by US Dollars and would like to see this system come to an end.

Even if it wanted to, the U.S. could never shut down all of the full nodes, even within its borders. How do you seize all of the computers that are running an open-source software program? Open source software is currently protected under the First Amendment in the U.S.

If you do try to shut down people running the software, someone can just fire up a new computer, download the Bitcoin software, and get up and running again. Bitcoin is more difficult to stop than cannabis or alcohol, both of which the U.S. government tried and failed to shut down. Let's not forget the fact that billionaires and Wall Street also love Bitcoin now, and they have the lobbying power to protect it.

The billionaire Chamath Palihapitiya already owns 1 million Bitcoin. Other billionaires like the Winklevoss twins have been scooping up Bitcoin and stashing it away in cold storage. Like all good money, Bitcoin is being hoarded and taken out of circulation. This process has accelerated in 2020, with the entrance of institutional investors into the game. Famous hedge fund managers like Paul Tudor Jones and Stanley Druckenmiller have been buying Bitcoin. The billionaire Michael Saylor bought 17,732 Bitcoins for himself and another 40,824 Bitcoins for his publicly traded company (MicroStrategy).

Anyone who tells you that Bitcoin is going to be banned in the U.S. has simply not been paying attention. Good luck getting legislators to ban something that U.S. billionaires and Wall Street love. Why would regulators allow U.S. banks to custody Bitcoin (as they did in 2020), if they were planning on making Bitcoin illegal?

Myth: Bitcoin has no value because anyone can easily create their own cryptocurrency.

Anyone can fork (copy) the Bitcoin software, but no one can fork the Bitcoin ecosystem. You can create your own cryptocurrency, but how are you going to persuade all of the full nodes, miners, developers, and investors to accept your new cryptocurrency? I can easily create my own social networking software, but it doesn't mean that I will be able to steal users from Facebook. The real value is in the network of people who interact with the software, rather than the software itself.

Myth: Bitcoin will be replaced by a competitor.

Bitcoin is a money protocol. The internet still runs on old protocols like TCP/IP, HTTP, and SMTP. In a perfect world they would be better, but they stick around because they are "good enough." Bitcoin does a really good job of securing value in a trustless, uncensorable manner. Bitcoin is "good enough." Facebook supplanted MySpace because it didn't cost anything to open up an account on both networks. It's impossible to store your savings simultaneously in Bitcoin and in a new competing cryptocurrency, without first selling off some of your Bitcoin and using it to purchase the new crypto.

Bitcoin is protected by its strong network effects. Buyers go to Amazon because that's where all of the sellers are; sellers go to Amazon because that's where all of the buyers are. Bitcoin has the largest market cap, highest security (highest hash rate), and highest liquidity of any cryptocurrency, which makes it an ideal candidate for institutional investors. This creates a virtuous circle where Bitcoin gets even larger and more secure, the more institutional investors buy it.

Bitcoin is good at doing some very basic things— storing value and making it possible to send that value anywhere in the world. If you added more bells and whistles, it would only increase the attack surface of Bitcoin. Over time, there will be additional layers built on top of Bitcoin (like the Lightning Network, for example). But the foundation will stay the same. Only Bitcoin offers this highly secure, neutral, global settlement layer.

Myth: Bitcoin has no intrinsic value because it is not backed by anything.

The US dollar has also not been backed by anything, since at least 1971 when the U.S. officially left the gold standard. Nevertheless, the US dollar still functions as money. Some people think that a commodity needs to have industrial or practical use to function as money. This was certainly true of gold and sea-shells in the past (both could be used to make beautiful jewelry).

Humanity is now rapidly moving into the digital age, where we spend most of our waking hours in virtual worlds like social media and gaming. The younger generations intuitively get that Bitcoin fits in perfectly in this new digital existence. Bitcoin is easy to store and to send, and it is the best store of value available. You cannot make a necklace out of Bitcoin, but Millennials and Generation Z could care less.

Facebook also has no intrinsic value— it's just a bunch of 0's and 1's like Bitcoin. It's the network that has value— the fact that billions of people are willing to upload content and engage on the network. Bitcoin is also just a bunch of 0's and 1's, but it is "backed" (like Facebook) by the millions (and soon billions) of people who choose to interact with the network.

Anyone who says that something immaterial like software cannot be extremely valuable has clearly been asleep for the past 20 years.

Myth: Bitcoin is too volatile to be a good store of value.

Bitcoin is a truly free market. There is no central bank intervention, no circuit breakers or lock-limit down rules. Many people in 2020 have forgotten what a free market looks like.

When designing a currency, you can optimize for exchange rate stability (low volatility) or store of value, but not both. Bitcoin has a perfectly transparent monetary policy (no closed-door Federal Reserve meetings) and a fixed supply. The US dollar is not too volatile on a day-to-day basis, but it is losing its purchasing power every single year. Future Fed monetary policy is unknown, and the max supply of future US dollars is uncapped. The US Treasury and the Fed can "talk" the US dollar up or down over short periods of time, but US dollars are guaranteed to lose purchasing power over long periods of time.

In their early days, both Amazon and Apple's stocks were also extremely volatile. Their volatility has come down over time as their market caps have grown. If you waited for their stocks to become less volatile, you missed out on the entire 20-year run. Today, many people store their wealth in Amazon and Apple stock.

The same is true for Bitcoin. Its volatility has come down over time, though it is still more volatile than most assets. This is because there is such a limited supply of Bitcoin. Just like a low-float stock, small inflows and outflows to Bitcoin can move its price around a lot. As Bitcoin's market cap grows, larger and larger amounts of capital will be able to find a home in Bitcoin without moving its price around as much.

Right now, we can say that Bitcoin is an emerging store of value. It might not retain your purchasing power for 6 months, but it certainly has preserved purchasing power and even grown wealth spectacularly over longer time horizons.

People who want Bitcoin to be non-volatile but still have the potential to go up 100x from here are living in a dream world. High volatility is the price to be paid for ultra-high investment returns.

Fortunately, one can adjust one's position size in Bitcoin to take into account this volatility. A portfolio of just 1% Bitcoin and 99% cash has outperformed the S&P 500 over the past 10 years. If you put 1% of your portfolio in Bitcoin and it goes up 100x, you have just doubled your net worth. If you put 1% of your portfolio in Bitcoin and it goes to zero, you'll hardly notice.

I have found it best for myself to simply dollar cost average into Bitcoin over time. I buy some Bitcoin, lock it away in cold storage, and never look at the price. If you check the price of Bitcoin every hour, you will get seasick. Bitcoin is a like a Picasso painting— you should just buy it, hide it in your attic, and come back in a decade to check on the price.

Myth: Bitcoin can be hacked.

Bitcoin cannot be hacked using current technology. If you google "richest Bitcoin addresses," you will see list of public addresses that contain literally billions of dollars worth of Bitcoin. The Bitcoin is just sitting there out in the open, but no one can steal it. Bitcoin has never been successfully hacked. And it's not like people haven't tried. A billion-dollar bounty will pay for a group of the best hackers in the world. Bitcoin has been attacked many times, but has only gotten stronger. Quantum computers may be a threat to Bitcoin in the future, but they may also be used to defend the Bitcoin network. Anyone who doesn't invest in Bitcoin because of quantum computing is like a person who refuses to buy California real estate because the whole state will be underwater in a few thousand years.

If you leave your Bitcoin on any cryptocurrency exchange, it can be stolen. That's what happened at Mt. Gox. The Bitcoin was not itself hacked, but was stolen from account holders. Never leave your Bitcoin on a crypto exchange. "Not your keys, not your coins" is something that we will discuss extensively in the next chapter.

Myth: Bitcoin is not scalable. Bitcoin is not good for payments because the fees are too high.

This critique often comes from scammers who want you to buy their own cryptocurrency instead of Bitcoin. You'll often hear them say "Bitcoin can only do 7 transactions per second, while my coin can do a bazillion transactions per second." In the early days of Bitcoin, many people believed that Bitcoin's destiny was to be a sort of global, low-cost PayPal. Their emphasis was on Bitcoin as a payment system.

As time has passed, the "Bitcoin as store of value" narrative has won out. Like gold coins, Bitcoin is simply too valuable to be used in daily transactions. It functions much better as a secure settlement layer and store of value. There is no reason that we will ever need to use Bitcoin to buy a cup of coffee. That transaction size is handled fine by Visa or PayPal or Square. In the future, central bank digital currencies (CBDC's or "FedCoin") may provide the main payment rails for the financial system.

Either way, Bitcoin is limited by transaction speed, but not by transaction size. Those 7 transactions every second can be $100 each, or $100 billion each. In this way, it is very easy for Bitcoin to scale. At the end of each day, Square can aggregate the hundreds of millions of transactions that happened that day, and do one big transaction to settle it to the Bitcoin blockchain.

The best thing about Bitcoin is that it is a neutral, apolitical asset that is not issued or controlled by any government. This makes it ideal to serve as the global settlement layer for international banking, payments, and trade. Right now, the US dollar and US Treasuries are the main reserve asset held by foreign central banks. In the old days, the main reserve asset was gold, and in the future it may very well be "digital gold" or Bitcoin.

Bitcoin transaction fees are entirely driven by supply and demand. In the future, they will certainly rise as transaction sizes continue to rise. But for now, they are still extremely reasonable. Someone recently sent over $1 billion worth of Bitcoin and paid only $3 in transaction fees. Bitcoin blockchain space is extremely limited and valuable. Promoters of other cryptocurrencies who tout their low transaction fees fail to point out that these fees are low simply because there is not a lot of demand for the product (i.e. having your transaction included in their blockchain). Anyone who wants to send $1 billion is not going to use a lesser-known cryptocurrency simply because it has lower fees. When you are sending large amounts of money, you want the highest security possible, and are willing to pay higher fees for it.

Myth: Bitcoin's max supply of 21 million coins will eventually be increased.

While it is impossible to know the future, increasing the 21 million cap would dilute the wealth of current Bitcoin holders. Why would they ever agree to such a thing?

You would need agreement from a lot of different parties to change the Bitcoin maximum supply by changing the software code: miners, full nodes, developers, Bitcoin holders, etc.

A lot of people who are new to Bitcoin don't recognize the important role that is played by full nodes on the Bitcoin network. Full nodes are simply computers around the world that are running the Bitcoin software and using it to ensure that the Bitcoin rules are being followed by miners and other participants. Full nodes each possess a full copy of the Bitcoin blockchain—that's why they are called "full." The Bitcoin blockchain is simply a record of all Bitcoin transactions that have taken place since 2009. The blockchain is a public, open ledger that can be viewed by anyone who downloads the Bitcoin software. Anyone can view this blockchain, but no one can alter it, as we shall see.

The Bitcoin blockchain is just a series of "blocks" that have been linked together. When a new Bitcoin transaction occurs (I send you 1 Bitcoin), it is added to the next block in the Bitcoin blockchain. A block is just a collection of recent transactions that have been verified and securely recorded. A new block is produced ("mined") approximately every 10 minutes, and added to the blockchain. The Bitcoin blockchain is currently about 316 gigabytes.

Every full node is watching these new blocks being produced, and making sure that they are not violating the software code. The blocks are not allowed to be too big, and they mustn't spend the same Bitcoin twice (the double-spending problem). The full nodes also watch to make sure that the 21 million max supply cap is never violated.

Many serious Bitcoiners run a full node. If you own Bitcoin, you are incentivized to make sure that your position is never diluted by having that 21 million cap raised. If it is raised to 25 million, your holdings of Bitcoin get diluted and are not worth as much.

So you could modify the Bitcoin software to increase the supply of coins past 21 million, but you would have a very difficult time getting anyone (whether full nodes or miners or Bitcoin holders) to run this new version of the software. It would run counter to their own financial interests. All full nodes are equal in the Bitcoin network. No full node has any special privileges or rights that the others do not.

Myth: Bitcoin was designed by the U.S. government or some other government to enslave people.

Nothing could be further from the truth. The U.S. government has never invented anything of value, and has proven itself strangely incompetent at even trying to move snail mail around the country or setting up a simple website (the doomed Obamacare website launch). The U.S. government still has a monopoly on currency, and would never invent an open-source software that would eventually endanger that monopoly.

Bitcoin is the money version of free speech. It cannot be censored or stopped. You can send a payment to anyone in the world, and Bitcoin doesn't care about your nationality, race, or politics. Bitcoin will never freeze your account like PayPal. Bitcoin doesn't look down on you like Goldman Sachs. And Bitcoin will never dilute your savings like the Federal Reserve does.

4

HOW TO BUY AND STORE BITCOIN

What's the best way to buy and store Bitcoin?

Some people use PayPal or Robinhood. I personally don't like those services, because they do not allow you to withdraw your Bitcoin and hold it in cold storage.

Here is the most important principle to remember when buying Bitcoin:

> **If you do not hold your own private keys, the Bitcoin is not really yours.**

If someone else holds your private keys (like PayPal, Robinhood, or any cryptocurrency exchange), you do not control your own Bitcoin. The Bitcoin does not truly belong to you. It can be lost, hacked, seized, or otherwise confiscated. If you buy Bitcoin using PayPal and they decide to freeze your account, you're out of luck. There's a common saying among Bitcoiners:

> **"Not your keys, not your coins."**

If you need to log in to an account to view your Bitcoin, it probably means that someone else is holding your private keys for you. That someone else is called a "third party custodian."

On the other hand, if you hold your Bitcoin on a hardware wallet (like a Trezor), it means that you are holding your own private keys.

Let me explain. In Bitcoin, you have public addresses and private keys. The public address is like an email address, where you can receive Bitcoin. It is safe to give someone your Bitcoin public address, if you would like them to send you some Bitcoin. It is possible to view how much Bitcoin is being held at a public address, but impossible to steal the Bitcoin from that address unless you know the private key associated with that Bitcoin public address. A Bitcoin public address will look something like this:

3J98t1WpEZ73CNmQviecrnyiWrnqRhWNLy

Your hardware wallet will be able to generate new public addresses whenever you need them. It's best practice not to reuse public addresses, since they can be tracked by blockchain analysis firms.

So that's how a Bitcoin **public address** works. A Bitcoin **private key** is like a password to your email or other account. You would never share your password with anyone, and likewise you should never share your private key. You should also never take a picture of it, or upload it online.

Your Bitcoin private key "unlocks" the Bitcoin that is sitting at your Bitcoin public address and allows you to move it. Your Bitcoin is not stored on your computer hard drive, or on your phone, or inside of your hardware wallet. It is actually "stored" on the Bitcoin blockchain itself, copies of which are found anywhere in the world where someone is running a full node. The amount of Bitcoin that you own is stored at a particular public address (or multiple addresses) on the blockchain, and can be unlocked/moved/spent by "signing" with your private key. A Bitcoin private key will look something like this:

E9873D79C6D87DC0FB6A5778633389F4453213303DA61F20BD67FC233

It is a 64-character hexadecimal number that unlocks your Bitcoin and allows you to send it anywhere. You might want to send your Bitcoin to a merchant to spend it, or send it to a cryptocurrency exchange like Coinbase to sell it for USD or EUR.

Note that I just took that Bitcoin public address and Bitcoin private key from a quick Google search. Please do not try to use them or send any Bitcoin to that public address. I have no idea if it even exists, or who controls it if it does exist.

You also don't want to leave your private key printed out on a piece of paper next to your desk, or put it into an email. If anyone gets their hands on your private key, they can move your Bitcoin to their own public address, and you will no longer have access to it. Unfortunately, the private key is a very long number that's virtually impossible to memorize, and yet too dangerous to store online. So what is one to do?

The best solution is to use a hardware wallet (like a Trezor). A hardware wallet is a physical device that looks a little bit like a USB flash drive (usually with a small screen). It connects to the USB port on your computer, and allows you to safely hold your Bitcoin private keys offline. It is the best solution that I have found for safely storing Bitcoin private keys. A hardware wallet serves two main functions:

1. It stores your private keys offline, and allows you to "sign" a Bitcoin transaction using those private keys whenever you want to unlock and move your Bitcoin.
2. It functions as a backup mechanism for your private keys. When you first set up your hardware wallet, it will allow you to generate a backup (called a "recovery seed") of your private keys that can be used in case your hardware wallet is destroyed by flood or fire, or otherwise lost.

Hardware wallets are examples of what are often called "cold wallets." They are not connected to the internet, and most of the time they are not even connected to your computer. You should always unplug your hardware wallet from your computer when you are done signing with it.

"Hot wallets" are Bitcoin wallets that are connected to the internet. You are probably using a hot wallet if you downloaded a wallet app on your phone, or on your laptop browser.

Hot wallets, because they are connected to the internet, are much less secure. They are prone to being hacked. Think of your hot wallet like your purse or leather wallet. You would probably never store more than $200 or so in your leather wallet, and you should treat your Bitcoin hot wallet the same way. Hot wallets are for spending and receiving small amounts of Bitcoin (whatever "small" means to you). If you wouldn't walk around with it inside of your leather wallet, you probably should not be keeping it on a hot wallet.

Cold wallets like the Trezor are best for storing larger amounts of Bitcoin that you planning on holding as a long-term investment.

We're now finally in a position to talk about how to buy and store Bitcoin. I like to use the cryptocurrency exchange Coinbase Pro to buy my Bitcoin. After buying it, I immediately withdraw the Bitcoin and hold it on a hardware wallet like the Trezor. The Cash App (by Square) will also allow you to buy Bitcoin using your phone and withdraw it to a hardware wallet.

I should mention that I'm not affiliated with or paid by any company that I mention in this book. Coinbase has terrible customer service, but then so do all of the other cryptocurrency exchanges that I've dealt with.

To get started, you just open up an account with Coinbase (Gemini and Kraken are also fine in the U.S.). You'll have to provide your personal information and Social Security number, which is required by all U.S. regulated cryptocurrency exchanges due to KYC/AML regulations ("Know Your Customer" and "Anti-Money Laundering").

Once your Coinbase account is open, you can move US dollars into it from your regular bank account. Coinbase will allow you to link to your bank account, so that you can "ACH" ("automated clearing house") some money over to Coinbase. You can also wire money into your Coinbase account, if you want to get started sooner. An ACH transfer will normally take 3-5 business days, while a wire should take less than 24 hours to clear.

Wait until your cash settles at Coinbase before placing a trade. Coinbase will allow you to buy Bitcoin immediately after you move money in, but you will not be able to withdraw that Bitcoin until your ACH or wire settles. If you buy Bitcoin before your cash settles, you will have to leave it in your Coinbase account and will not be able to withdraw it until your cash settles. While you are waiting for this, there is the risk that Coinbase could get hacked and your Bitcoin could be stolen.

Yes, Coinbase does carry insurance, but read the fine print. If there is a large hack, there is a good chance that the insurance will not cover the total amount of Bitcoin stolen, and you will only receive a partial recovery.

I've used both Coinbase Pro and Gemini ActiveTrader, and both services currently have the lowest commissions/trading costs that I have seen (approximately 0.30% to 0.50%). By contrast, you'll pay more than 1.00% if you use the Cash App. The lower the fees, the more Bitcoin you will end up with at the end of the day.

Once you open up your account with Coinbase, just navigate here to the Coinbase Pro side to get lower commissions:

https://pro.coinbase.com/

Make sure that you don't buy garbage coins like BCH (Bitcoin Cash) or BSV (Bitcoin Satoshi's Vision). These are both failed offshoots ("forks") of Bitcoin (BTC) and will never make you any money. **The correct ticker will have BTC in it.** If you are buying Bitcoin (BTC) using US dollars in Coinbase Pro, the ticker is BTC-USD.

My favorite hardware wallet is the Trezor Model T (I'm not affiliated with or being compensated in any way by Trezor). It's not cheap at $170, but it might make sense if you are holding any significant amount of Bitcoin. Even if the value of your Bitcoin is relatively small right now, think about how you will feel if Bitcoin goes up 100x from here. Will you still be comfortable storing your Bitcoin with a third party custodian or on a hot wallet?

The Trezor wallet is open-source, which means that there are many eyes scanning the code worldwide and looking for possible bugs or other attack vectors. The Ledger hardware wallet is closed source, so I do not like it. Ledger also has a history of having its customer database hacked and spilled onto the internet, complete with home addresses! I like the ColdCard hardware wallet as well, but it is not as easy to set up as the Trezor.

Never buy a used hardware wallet, or buy a Trezor from a third-party source. If you do, the seller may have loaded some malware onto the Trezor that will allow him to remotely steal your Bitcoin. The fewer middlemen, the better for security.

When your Trezor comes in the mail, make sure that the package has not been opened, and that the tamper-evident holographic seal is still in place on the Trezor itself. When you first connect your Trezor to a USB port on your laptop or desktop, it will install the latest firmware. If it does not prompt you to do this installation, something may be wrong. An attacker may have already installed their own malware onto the Trezor. If this happens, contact Trezor support immediately.

Make sure that you are using the Chrome browser and that you go to this page before you plug in your Trezor:

https://trezor.io/start/

If you misspell this URL, you may be taken to a scammer site that looks similar, but that is set up to steal your Bitcoin. I've even seen these scammers advertise in the Google paid search results for Trezor.

Before you move any Bitcoin onto your Trezor, it is very important to generate a recovery seed. The Trezor website will give you this option when you first set up your Trezor hardware wallet. The recovery seed will be shown, one word at a time, on your Trezor screen, and you should use a pen and paper to write down these words in the order that they are given. Use a fresh sheet of paper, and make sure that the imprint of the words does not transfer to your desk surface or to the piece of paper directly underneath it when you write. Your recovery seed will look something like this:

1. abandon
2. ability
3. able
4. about
5. above
6. absent
7. absorb
8. abstract
9. absurd
10. abuse
11. access
12. accident

The words will be automatically selected from a pool of 2,048 English words that you can view here:

https://github.com/bitcoin/bips/blob/master/bip-0039/english.txt

The recovery seed is 12 or 24 English words in a particular order. Recording the order of these words, as I did above, is very important. The recovery seed is a representation of the private keys that are associated with your Trezor wallet. If your Trezor is ever lost or damaged, you can buy a new Trezor hardware wallet (or pretty much any hardware wallet that is on the BIP39 standard), and enter your recovery seed into the new wallet. Even if the Trezor company goes out of business, you can use your recovery seed to "reload" a hardware wallet that you purchase from a different hardware wallet company. Trezor the company will never be able to view your recovery seed, or how much Bitcoin is stored on your Trezor hardware wallet.

It is very important to remember:

Possession of your recovery seed= ownership of your Bitcoin

For this reason, it is very important to hide your recovery seed in a safe place and make multiple backups of it. Never share your recovery seed with anyone that you don't trust. Some people like to laminate the piece of paper that has their recovery seed written on it and store it in a fireproof and waterproof home safe. You can check out the CypherWheel or similar devices if you want to store your recovery seed on a metal device that is fireproof and rustproof.

Here are some important rules to follow when it comes to your recovery seed:

- Never put your recovery seed into an email, or enter it into any online form in your browser. It should only be entered directly onto your Trezor device.
- Never take a picture of your recovery seed, or upload it to the cloud.
- Never keep your recovery seed on your laptop or desktop computer.
- Never store your recovery seed anywhere online, including Evernote or Google Drive.
- Put a piece of dark tape over your computer camera when you are writing down your recovery seed.
- Do not whisper the words in your recovery seed when you are writing them down.

- Generate and write down your recovery seed in a completely private room, without your smartphone present.

If you hold very small amounts of Bitcoin (relative to your total net worth), it's probably fine to keep your Bitcoin on an exchange like Coinbase or in the Cash App. Don't let the complexity of storing Bitcoin prevent you from getting started. If you only have $100 worth of Bitcoin, it might not make financial sense to spend $170 on a hardware wallet. The first step is to "get off of zero" and no longer be a "no-coiner."

As your holdings of Bitcoin grow, learn how to move your Bitcoin off of Coinbase Pro and onto a hardware wallet like the Trezor. Get comfortable moving your Bitcoin back and forth between Coinbase Pro and your Trezor hardware wallet. Send small test amounts at first, so that if you make a mistake, you won't be out too much money. Every time you move your Bitcoin around, you will be charged a small transaction fee that gets paid directly to a Bitcoin miner. These transaction fees will vary, depending on supply and demand for Bitcoin blockspace at the time.

As your holdings of Bitcoin grow even more, consider moving to a multisig ("multisignature") storage solution. This is a safer way of storing your Bitcoin that requires multiple signatures from different hardware wallets to move your Bitcoin. It removes the single point of failure problem that is present with single hardware wallets.

I am currently using a multisig solution to store my Bitcoin. I don't keep any hardware wallets or recovery seeds at my house or on my person, so please don't come looking for them or for me. People know that I own Bitcoin, and so I've had to take multiple security precautions. If you want to stalk a Bitcoiner, there are better targets than me. I'm nowhere close to being a "Bitcoin whale."

If you want to learn more about how I store my Bitcoin using multisig, I've created a short video here:

https://www.youtube.com/watch?v=dt7mryC8kLQ&ab_channel=TraderUniversity

THE 10 COMMANDMENTS OF BITCOIN

1. Value your wealth in Bitcoin
2. Dollar cost average into Bitcoin
3. Never sell your Bitcoin
4. Never trade in and out of Bitcoin
5. Ignore the price of Bitcoin
6. Not your keys, not your coins
7. Never share your recovery seed
8. Don't advertise your Bitcoin holdings
9. Ignore all other cryptocurrencies
10. You can never be too bullish on Bitcoin.

1. **Value your wealth in Bitcoin.** Focus on accumulating as many Bitcoin as possible, and ignore their value in your local currency. Stop translating your Bitcoin holdings back into dollars. Try to collect Bitcoin ("stack sats"), just like you would collect rare baseball cards, or rare cars, or rare art. You don't check the value of your house every day. You shouldn't check the value of your Bitcoin every day either. Start thinking in terms of Bitcoin and using it as your unit of account. Value your wealth in Bitcoin.

2. **Dollar cost average into Bitcoin.** Buy $100 (or whatever amount works best for you) every week on the same day and at the same time. Don't risk money that you cannot afford to lose. Consult a financial advisor before taking any action. Don't try to time Bitcoin's peaks and troughs. Don't have FOMO (fear of missing out). Just stack sats every day and stay humble. Buy your Bitcoin using an exchange like Coinbase.

Don't try to mine your own Bitcoin. As we mentioned before, Bitcoin mining has become a very specialized and competitive industry. It is strictly for the professionals, who can afford expensive mining machines (ASICs) and who have a cheap source of electricity. There is no longer any way for you to mine Bitcoin profitably from your laptop or phone. You will lose less money setting up a gold mine in your backyard. Run the opposite direction from all online "cloud mining" schemes.

3. Never sell your Bitcoin. Selling Bitcoin means capital gains taxes today, as well as missing out on Bitcoin's massive upside potential. Never sell your Bitcoin to buy stocks or real estate that will not go up as much as Bitcoin. Think about all the people who sold their Malibu beach houses or Picasso paintings (both extremely scarce assets, but not as scarce as Bitcoin) in 1950. Think about the future wealth that their descendants missed out on. Never ever sell your Bitcoin. Don't let anyone make you panic. Don't sell your Bitcoin and buy a depreciating asset like a car. In the future, it will be easy to borrow against your Bitcoin holdings to buy a house or something similar. This is what billionaires do— they often borrow against their stock holdings, instead of selling them.

4. Never trade in and out of Bitcoin. If an asset is going to go up 10x or 100x (or even more), there is no way that you will be able to get higher returns by trading in and out. It's more likely that you'll sell at the wrong time, and not know when to get back in. It's not about timing the market, but time in the market. Don't try to trade other cryptocurrencies as a way of eventually getting more Bitcoin. You are guaranteed to mess up the timing. If you want more Bitcoin, buy more Bitcoin.

5. Ignore the price of Bitcoin. Value your wealth in Bitcoin, not USD or EUR or YEN. There is no reason to be checking the price of Bitcoin every few hours if you are planning on holding it for 10 years— or forever. If you do check the price, you might get greedy and sell; or you might get scared and sell. Better to ignore the price fluctuations and volatility, unless you enjoy roller coasters or getting seasick. Get a life and get off your phone. Spend time with your kids and loved ones.

6. Not your keys, not your coins. Don't buy Bitcoin using PayPal or Robinhood or any other service that will not allow you to withdraw your Bitcoin to a hardware wallet. Never let anyone hold your private keys for you, or leave your Bitcoin on a cryptocurrency exchange (like Coinbase, Gemini, Kraken, etc.— none of them are safe).

7. Never share your recovery seed. Never put your recovery seed in an email, in Evernote or a Google doc, or upload it anywhere online. Never take a picture of it with your smartphone. Put a piece of tape over your computer's webcam when you are writing down your recovery seed. Do not write down your recovery seed in a public space, like a Starbuck's. Do not whisper your recovery seed words while you are writing them down. Never enter your recovery seed into an online form. If anyone has your recovery seed, they now control your Bitcoin.

8. Don't advertise your Bitcoin holdings to the world. Only tell close trusted family members or friends. Don't put it on a vanity license plate, or otherwise make yourself a kidnapping or ransom target.

9. Ignore all other cryptocurrencies. Bitcoin is the next Bitcoin. Most other cryptocurrencies are scams or pump and dumps that are designed to enrich insiders. If you're not a cryptographer or advanced software developer who can read cryptocurrency source code, ignore everything except Bitcoin.

10. You can never be too bullish on Bitcoin. Bitcoin will be much bigger than anyone can imagine. Bitcoin is the best store of value in the world. It is slowly eating the world, and demonetizing other stores of value, like gold, stocks, and real estate. Bitcoin is digital gold. It is like gold, but much better. Bitcoin is scarcer, and easier to verify, store, and send. "Store of value" is the biggest use case in the solar system. Bitcoin will eat the world— the whole world, and then move on to the planets. It is the biggest investment opportunity in a thousand years.

6

THE BITCOIN REVOLUTION IS HERE

I hope that you've enjoyed this book and that you too will be able to participate in the Bitcoin revolution. We are blessed to live in very exciting times. Things are moving ever faster in this global and digital economy. You can be sure that the world will have already changed before the ink on this book is dry. Thanks for purchasing this book and reading it all the way to the end.

If you enjoyed this book and found it useful, I'd be very grateful if you'd post an honest review on Amazon.

Just go to www.trader-books.com and click on "A Beginner's Guide to Bitcoin." Then click the blue link next to the yellow stars that says "ratings." You will then see a gray button on the left-hand side of the page that says "Write a customer review"— click that and you're good to go.

If you would like to learn more ways to make money in the markets, be sure to also check out my other books on the next page.

DISCLAIMER

While the author has used his best efforts in preparing this book, he makes no representations or warranties with respect to the accuracy or completeness of the contents of this book and specifically disclaims any implied warranties or merchantability or fitness for a particular purpose. The advice and strategies contained herein may not be suitable for your situation.

You should consult with a legal, financial, tax, or other professional where appropriate. Neither the publisher nor the author shall be liable for any loss of profit or any other commercial damages, including but not limited to special, incidental, consequential, or other damages.

This book is for educational purposes only. The views expressed are those of the author alone, and should not be taken as expert instruction or commands. The reader is responsible for his or her own actions.

Adherence to all applicable laws and regulations, including international, federal, state, and local laws, is the sole responsibility of the purchaser or reader.

Neither the author nor the publisher assumes any responsibility or liability whatsoever on the behalf of the purchaser or reader of these materials.

Any perceived slight of any individual or organization is purely unintentional.

Past performance is not necessarily indicative of future performance.

Forex, futures, stock, and options trading is not appropriate for everyone.

Futures and forex trading contain substantial risk and are not for every investor. An investor could potentially lose all or more than the initial investment. Risk capital is money that can be lost without jeopardizing ones' financial security or life style. Only risk capital should be used for trading and only those with sufficient risk capital should consider trading. Past performance is not necessarily indicative of future results.

There is a substantial risk of loss associated with trading these markets. Losses can and will occur. No system or methodology has ever been developed that can guarantee profits or ensure freedom from losses. Nor will it likely ever be.

No representation or implication is being made that using the methodologies or systems or the information contained within this book will generate profits or ensure freedom from losses.

The information contained in this book is for educational purposes only and should NOT be taken as investment advice. Examples presented here are not solicitations to buy or sell. The author, publisher, and all affiliates assume no responsibility for your trading results.

There is a high risk in trading.

HYPOTHETICAL OR SIMULATED PERFORMANCE RESULTS HAVE CERTAIN LIMITATIONS.

UNLIKE AN ACTUAL PERFORMANCE RECORD, SIMULATED RESULTS DO NOT REPRESENT ACTUAL TRADING. ALSO, SINCE THE TRADES HAVE NOT BEEN EXECUTED, THE RESULTS MAY HAVE UNDER-OR-OVER COMPENSATED FOR THE IMPACT, IF ANY, OF CERTAIN MARKET FACTORS, SUCH AS THE LACK OF LIQUIDITY.

SIMULATED TRADING PROGRAMS IN GENERAL ARE ALSO SUBJECT TO THE FACT THAT THEY ARE DESIGNED WITH THE BENEFIT OF HINDSIGHT. NO REPRESENTATION IS BEING MADE THAT ANY ACCOUNT WILL OR IS LIKELY TO ACHIEVE PROFIT OR

LOSSES SIMILAR TO THOSE SHOWN.